TECHNOLOGY IN ACTION

CAMERA TECHNOLOGY

Alastair Jervis

The Bookwright Press
New York · 1991

Titles in this series

First published in the
United States in 1991 by
The Bookwright Press
387 Park Avenue South
New York, NY 10016

First published in 1990 by
Wayland (Publishers) Ltd
61 Western Road, Hove
East Sussex BN3 1JD, England

Front cover The Nikon F4 is one of today's most sophisticated autofocus SLRs, combining tried and tested mechanical features with the latest in computer technology.

Library of Congress Cataloging-in-Publication Data
Jervis, Alastair.
   Camera technology / by Alastair Jervis.
   p.   cm. (Technology in action.)
   Includes bibliographical references and index.
   Summary: An overview of the camera's
   development from the early 19th century
   experiments to the advances in technology of the
   late 20th century.
   ISBN 0-531-18385-8
   1. Cameras — Juvenile literature.
   [1. Cameras. 2. Photography.]
   I. Title. II. Series.
   TR149.J47   1991
   771.3—dc20   90-44515
                                                          CIP
                                                          AC

Typeset by Direct Image Photosetting Limited,
Sussex, England
Printed in Italy by G. Canale & C.S.p.A., Turin

Contents

Photography today

Nowadays, photographs are part of our lives. Besides vacation snapshots and pictures of family and friends that we enjoy taking, photographs help shape our understanding of the world around us. Pictures printed in newspapers, which can be transmitted from one part of the world to another in a matter of seconds, bring home to us the importance of historic events as they are happening; and we are all influenced by the advertising photographs we see in magazines and on billboards and posters. Photography also plays an important role in the modern scientific world; for instance, researchers are able to record on film the minute cell structures they see through their microscope lenses.

The cameras that produce all these images have operated on the same principles for decades, but technological advances have made modern cameras much more accurate and a great deal easier to use than earlier ones. The type of non-specialist camera that can be bought in any camera store today is small and portable, and, generally, it has sophisticated electronic systems that ensure that the picture comes out correctly. These automatic systems decide how much light should be allowed to reach the film at the back of the camera and

Today's cameras produce good quality pictures and are easy to use, making it possible for millions of people to enjoy photography.

then let in precisely that amount of light. A tiny, built-in motor winds the film forward after each picture and, in many cases, the camera's lens is focused automatically. These types of cameras often have built-in flashguns that are fired automatically in low light.

The advances in camera technology have made it possible for photography to be enjoyed by billions of people around the world. Not only are cameras becoming increasingly easy to use, the quality of the pictures they produce has never been better. While electronic video systems are certainly growing in importance – a number of still video cameras, in which a picture is recorded electronically rather than on photographic film have recently been launched – their pictures are not as sharp nor as detailed as those produced by conventional cameras. Photography seems set to remain the world's most important mass art form for some time to come.

Photographs provide a unique kind of information. This can range from instant news pictures of the 1990 release of Nelson Mandela (above) to precise scientific pictures of human red blood cells (below).

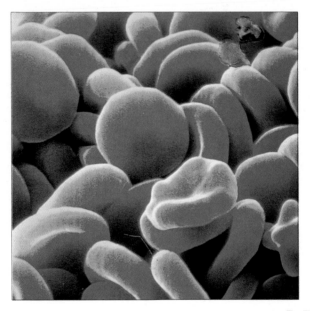

There are usually three, but sometimes only two, stages in the process of making a photograph – releasing the shutter, developing the film and printing the negative. The camera itself is involved in the first stage only, when light comes in through the lens and reaches the light-sensitive film at the back of the camera. At this stage, there is no visible effect on the film; it is only when the film has been developed in special chemicals that an image can be seen. Usually, the image that is formed is negative – one in which light areas of the original subject, such as the sky, are almost black, and dark areas appear as clear film. To produce a positive image, the negative has to be printed onto photographic paper in a lightproof darkroom.

For the negative to be good enough to print from, there are two important functions the camera must perform. First, its lens must be adjusted so that it focuses light waves coming into the camera precisely. Second, the camera must be able to control the exposure. The exposure is determined by both the intensity of the light coming into the camera and the length of time that the film is exposed to the light. To control the first of these factors, all except the most basic camera lenses have a variable diaphragm. This is a roughly circular-shaped opening in the lens which can be made smaller or larger to reduce or increase the amount of light entering the camera. The size of the opening is called the aperture.

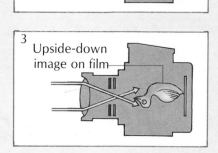

These three diagrams illustrate the basic principles of photography.

1 Rays of light from the subject being photographed enter the camera and are directed by the lens.

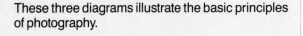

2 The rays of light pass through the open diaphragm.

3 An inverted image is focused on the film at the back of the camera.

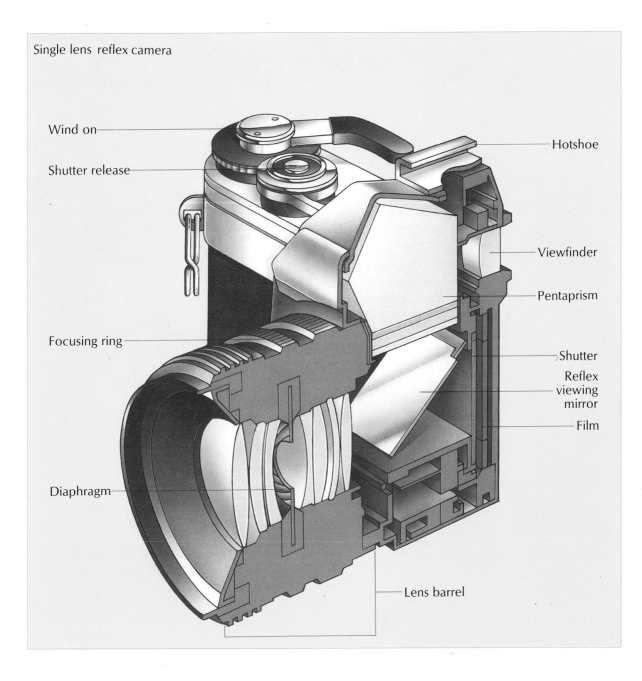

Single lens reflex camera

Wind on

Shutter release

Hotshoe

Viewfinder

Pentaprism

Focusing ring

Shutter

Reflex
viewing
mirror

Film

Diaphragm

Lens barrel

The length of time that the film is exposed to the light is controlled by the camera's shutter. This forms a barrier between the light coming into the camera and the film. The shutter opens only when the button on top of the camera is pressed, allowing the light to reach the film. Because most of the films we use today are very sensitive to light, these shutters must be able to open and close at very fast speeds.

The advanced, modern camera does, of course, have other functions, the most important of which are a system for measuring the exposure and a viewfinder through which the photographer can see what the picture will look like. Every camera also has to have some means of winding the film forward after each picture has been taken. This might be either a crank on its top plate or a built-in motor.

It has been known for centuries that an image of a scene can be produced by allowing light to pass through a small hole or a glass lens. By the seventeenth century, artists were using portable boxes fitted with a lens and a mirror to help them in their work. Light passed through the lens, which focused it into an image (that was upside-down), and this was reflected by the mirror onto a drawing board. The artist could then trace the image. This device was known as the camera obscura (meaning "darkened room"), or pinhole camera, and many different designs of it were used.

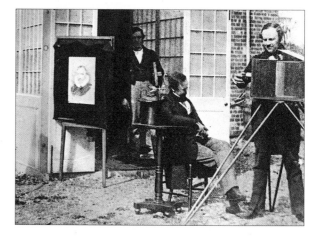

Below The camera obscura. An image was produced by allowing light through a tiny hole.

Above William Henry Fox Talbot at work. The pictures produced were called calotypes.

Above This print produced in 1824 by Nicéphore Niépce is one of the oldest surviving photographs. No one had previously been able to ''fix'' an image permanently.

Why then did it take so long for the photographic camera to come into existence? A way of making the image created in the camera obscura permanent, ''fixing'' it, had to be found, and this discovery marked the beginning of photography as we know it.

Photography is generally said to have been invented in 1839, but the first real photograph was produced some fifteen years earlier by a Frenchman named Nicéphore Niépce. Using a metal plate coated with a light-sensitive material, in a camera obscura, Niépce managed to record a view from his window. The exposure took eight hours. However, it was in 1839 that photography really became a practical process. It was then that the Frenchman Louis Daguerre and the Englishman William Henry Fox Talbot revealed to the world their different systems for recording a permanent image produced by a camera.

Above Niépce's first camera. All early cameras had to be supported on a stand or table.

Above The daguerreotype camera was a simple wooden box with a lens on the front. This focused an image onto a light-sensitive plate at the back of the camera.

Above Louis Daguerre. At first, his process proved more popular than Fox Talbot's.

The processes of Fox Talbot and Daguerre differed in the way in which the image was fixed, but the cameras used were very similar. They were basically large wooden boxes with a simple lens, always supported on a tripod. There was no need for shutters or diaphragms, because the exposures required for a recognizable picture to be made took several minutes. The lens could simply be uncovered and then covered again once the exposure was complete. This made life very uncomfortable for those people who rushed to have their portraits taken in the fashionable new photographic studios: their necks were held in clamps to stop them from blurring the picture by moving their heads during the exposure.

The images produced by these early cameras, and most of the ones that followed soon after, were much larger than the negatives we get from most modern cameras – a common size was 5 × 3 in (13 × 8 cm). Although this made the

The flexible leather bellows of these cameras allow the lens to be moved forward
or backward for focusing.

cameras very large and awkward to use, it was essential because there were no means of enlarging the images: the size of the light-sensitive plate at the back of the camera was the size of the finished picture.

Although we are now used to much smaller cameras, equipment that is very similar to these early devices is still used by some photo-graphers today. View, or sheet-film cameras consist of two panels, connected by a flexible, lightproof leather bellows, which are mounted on a third panel. The front panel contains the lens, the shutter and the diaphragm; the back panel has a ground-glass screen through which the photographer views the subject. Moving the two panels closer together or farther apart

focuses the image. When the photographer is ready to take the picture, a single sheet of film is loaded into the back panel and the shutter is released to let in the light. The camera has to be reloaded every time a picture is taken.

By modern standards, these cameras are unsophisticated and very difficult to use, but they do have one crucial advantage: the quality of the pictures produced cannot be bettered. When very big prints are required, the negatives made by sheet-film cameras need much less enlargement than negatives from smaller cameras, so the final image shows less grain. For this reason, sheet-film cameras are often used to supply pictures that are to be displayed on advertising billboards.

In the early years of this century, most photographers were using cameras that produced pictures about 3 × 2 in (8 × 6 cm) in size. The cameras no longer had to be reloaded constantly because rolls of film were available by then, but the size of the equipment was still something of a hindrance.

The first stage in the camera design revolution took place in 1914. Oscar Barnack, a designer with the German microscope manufacturers Leitz, built a miniature camera for his own use. Barnack's camera used off-cuts from the 35mm-wide film that had been developed for the motion picture industry. Consequently, it was much smaller than other contemporary camera designs. Ten years later, Leitz began to produce an improved version of the camera commercially, calling it the Leica. And so 35mm photography was born.

The Leica was the first precision miniature camera, but it was not a single lens reflex (SLR), the type of camera that dominates 35mm photography today. The first mass-produced SLR was the Exacta, another German-made camera, which went on sale in the mid-1930s. Like all SLRs, the Exacta had at its heart a hinged mirror, called the reflex viewing mirror, angled at 45° to the path of the light coming into the camera. The image focused by the lens was reflected by the mirror up onto a ground-glass screen on the top plate, where it could be viewed by the photographer. When the shutter release was pressed, the mirror flipped up out of the light path and a shutter behind it opened to make the exposure.

The most important benefit of using mirrors in cameras is that the image seen through the viewfinder is the right way up instead of being upside-down, as it would be if the image was focused directly onto the viewfinder's glass screen. The viewfinder image is still, however,

An early SLR of the Graflex type.

reversed from left to right. To correct this, a pentaprism is built into the top of an SLR. This is a multi-sided, silvered prism that, through a series of reflections, turns the image the right way around in the viewfinder.

Above Today's SLRs are smooth and rounded in shape. In this model, the built-in flash unit is on top of the pentaprism.

Right These three diagrams show how the reflex viewing system works in an SLR.

It is this viewing system that defines the SLR camera. The vast majority of models also have the highly important feature that lenses can be detached from the camera. This means that the photographer can use any number of lenses of differing focal lengths with just one camera body. Because the image seen in the viewfinder is produced directly by the light coming through the lens, the photographer can see the effect of changing lenses immediately.

The single lens reflex is probably the closest photographic manufacturers have come to producing the perfect camera design, but it does have some important drawbacks. First, there is a limit to how much smaller SLRs can become, because there has to be enough room for the mirror to flip up, out of the light path.

The reflex viewing system

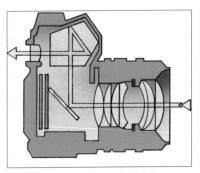

1 Light passes through the lens and is reflected by the mirror into the pentaprism and then the viewfinder. The aperture is at its widest setting.

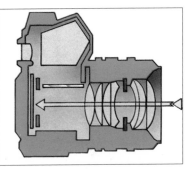

2 When the shutter is released, the mirror flips up and the light passes through the shutter to the film. The aperture is adjusted to whatever setting is needed.

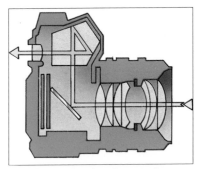

3 After the shot has been taken the mirror drops down and the aperture returns to its widest setting.

Second, the photographer cannot see through the viewfinder at the moment of exposure, because the mirror has been moved out of the light path. This makes "panning" (moving the camera to follow a moving subject while the exposure is taking place) difficult. Finally, and most important, the fact that the mirror has to move before the shutter can be opened results in a slight delay between the moment the shutter release is pressed and the making of the exposure. This delay can be critical for sports photographers trying to take pictures of fast-moving action.

The Japanese camera manufacturer Canon recently devised a solution to this problem.

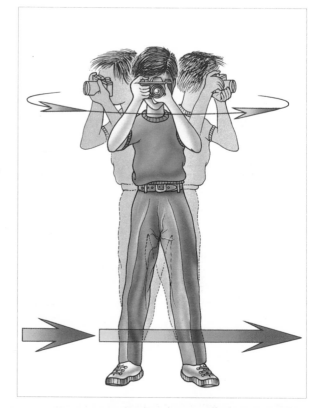

Right Expert photographers will often use a technique called "panning" when photographing fast-moving objects. The camera is swiveled so that the subject is kept in the same position in the viewfinder throughout the exposure. The result is a sharp image of the subject against a blurred background (below).

A medium-format Hasselblad camera from Sweden. The advantage of such cameras is that their larger negative size allows for better enlargements.

Canon's EOS RT camera incorporates a fixed pellicle mirror. This is a special mirror that reflects some of the light up into the viewfinder while allowing most of it to pass through to the film. As a result, the mirror does not have to be moved and the exposure is made the instant the shutter release button is pressed.

Most SLRs, nowadays, take 35mm film, but there are some that take film that is 6 cm wide and are known as medium-format cameras. These cameras are popular with professional photographers because the large negatives they produce offer better picture quality than 35mm negatives enlarged to the same size, but are small enough to be easily portable.

The earliest medium-format cameras had a twin lens design, and there are still a number of cameras of this type available today. In these cameras, one of the two lenses is linked to the viewfinder for focusing, and the other is the camera's "taking" lens. The two lenses are linked so that focusing adjustments are automatically transferred to the taking lens. Most modern medium-format cameras, however, use SLR design. In comparison with 35mm SLRs, they seem rather unsophisticated, with few, if any, electronic parts. This is another reason why they are popular with professional photographers, who cannot afford to have their cameras out of action because of battery failure.

The compact camera

Compact cameras differ from SLRs in two ways. First, their lenses are built into the camera body and, in almost all cases, cannot be detached; second, they use a direct viewing system. To compose a picture, the photographer looks through a small window above and to one side of the lens. Lines drawn in this viewfinder show the approximate area that will appear in the finished picture. This system does not require a mirror, so the cameras can be smaller than SLRs, but it does have one disadvantage. What the photographer sees in the viewfinder is not *exactly* what is taken by the lens. This fault, which is called parallax error, is particularly noticeable with close-up subjects, as you can see from the diagram.

Most compacts are designed to make photography as simple as possible for the camera owner. In this respect, they are the descendants of a camera produced over 100 years ago by an American named George Eastman.

Above Modern compacts like this are small and simple to use. One drawback is the problem of parallax error (below). The diagram shows how the distant frame (LB) is more like the image in the viewfinder than the close-up (LA).

Parallax error

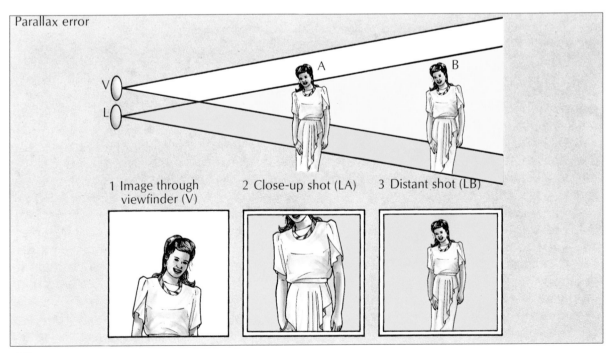

1 Image through viewfinder (V)

2 Close-up shot (LA)

3 Distant shot (LB)

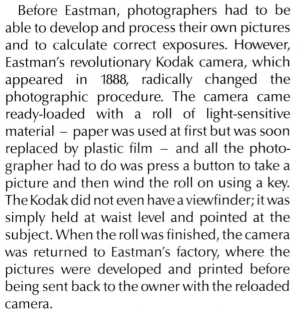

Before Eastman, photographers had to be able to develop and process their own pictures and to calculate correct exposures. However, Eastman's revolutionary Kodak camera, which appeared in 1888, radically changed the photographic procedure. The camera came ready-loaded with a roll of light-sensitive material – paper was used at first but was soon replaced by plastic film – and all the photographer had to do was press a button to take a picture and then wind the roll on using a key. The Kodak did not even have a viewfinder; it was simply held at waist level and pointed at the subject. When the roll was finished, the camera was returned to Eastman's factory, where the pictures were developed and printed before being sent back to the owner with the reloaded camera.

Today's compacts make it possible for people with little technical knowledge to enjoy photography, just as the Kodak did 100 years ago. They are very small and easy to handle, and the great advances in electronics have enabled camera manufacturers to make compacts with sophisticated systems that automatically control focusing, exposure, film forwarding and loading.

George Eastman (above) played an important role in making photography available to ordinary people. His Kodak camera (top) was sold ready-loaded and the pictures were developed by his company rather than by the photographer.

Built-in automatic flashguns are common, and a number of compacts contain a small quartz clock that enables the photographer to print the time and date on the pictures.

Although most compacts use 35mm film, smaller film sizes are sometimes used. There are also compacts that allow you to take three-dimensional pictures. These cameras have three or sometimes four separate lenses. Each lens takes a separate picture. The pictures are then combined using a special printing process to achieve the three-dimensional effect.

The most important recent development in compact camera technology has been the arrival of zoom cameras. The first model of this type was the Zoom 70, made by the Japanese company Pentax and launched in 1987.

A zoom lens allows the photographer to select an area of a subject as the focus of a picture without moving closer to or farther away from the scene. Zooming the lens forward or backward has the same effect as if the photographer moved closer to or farther away from the subject. The zoom cameras have a lens of this type built into the body. Although there are a few manual models, most zoom cameras have a tiny motor inside them to move the zoom backward or forward.

There is, however, a problem with having zoom lenses on compact cameras. The conventional compact viewfinder is separate from the camera lens, and so the effects of zooming the lens cannot be seen in the viewfinder. This means that the photographer cannot be sure what the picture will look like. This problem was solved in the Pentax Zoom 70 because the compact's simple window viewfinder was replaced by one designed like the zoom lens itself. The motor that is used to zoom the lens in and out operates the viewfinder as well.

There is, of course, another solution, and that is to use a reflex viewing system, in which the viewfinder image comes through the lens itself. Cameras using this system are sometimes known as bridge cameras, because they bridge the gap between SLRs and compacts. The most advanced bridge cameras, such as the Ricoh Mirai, have all the advantages of the SLR except that their lenses cannot be detached from the camera body. The price that is paid for this is that the cameras are becoming larger and heavier. Unlike conventional compact cameras, they cannot be slipped into a pocket and carried anywhere.

This Pentax zoom camera has a focal length range of 38-105mm. The lens is zoomed in and out by a small motor, controlled by buttons on the back of the camera.

These two photographs, taken from the same position, show the effect of changing the focal length of the camera's zoom lens. The picture above was taken with the lens set to its maximum telephoto setting. With the lens set to a wide-angle focal length (left), far more can be included in the picture, but everything is much smaller.

The lens

A camera's lens bends the light waves coming from each single point of the subject being photographed making them converge (focusing them) on the film at some distance behind the lens.

The simplest camera lens is a single piece of ground glass with curved sides. Lenses of this sort are sometimes used in the least expensive modern cameras, but they are affected by a number of optical errors called "aberrations." More advanced modern lenses are made with something like eight pieces of glass, called "elements." The elements are of different shapes, so the light waves are bent both inward and outward before eventually being brought into focus. This helps to prevent aberrations from spoiling the finished picture.

Above Telephoto lenses like this can make subjects hundreds of yards away appear close.

Below The elements of a lens.

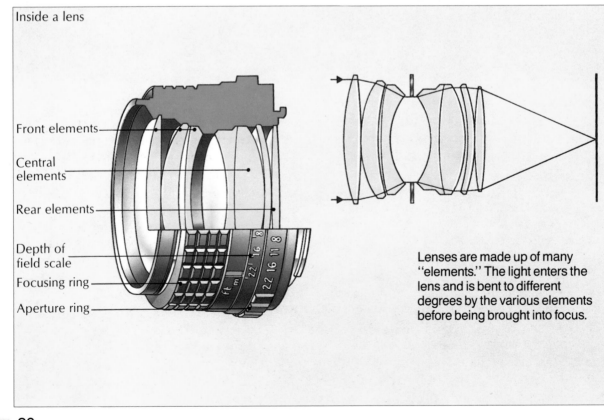

Inside a lens

Front elements

Central elements

Rear elements

Depth of field scale

Focusing ring

Aperture ring

Lenses are made up of many "elements." The light enters the lens and is bent to different degrees by the various elements before being brought into focus.

Fisheye lenses take in very wide scenes, but they also cause unusual effects. Here, for instance, the horizon appears curved.

The danger with having a large number of elements is that they will reduce the amount of light that reaches the film. In addition, some of the light can be reflected from all the glass surfaces and not be brought into focus at all. So, to prevent light from being lost or reflected, lens-makers coat the elements with a very fine layer of special chemicals.

The strength with which a lens bends light determines its focal length. The focal length is the distance between the lens and the focused image. A standard lens, which has a focal length of about 50mm, gives a view that is similar to that of human eyes and has always been a popular type of lens. Lenses with greater bending power have shorter focal lengths – 28mm and 35mm are common examples – and are called wide-angle lenses because they take in a broad area and focus it on the film. The opposite type of lens is called a telephoto lens. This takes in a much narrower area, so distant subjects can be photographed without being just tiny dots in the finished picture.

In recent times, computer technology has revolutionized lens design. Aberrations have been greatly reduced and more and more extreme focal lengths have been made possible. Wide-angle lenses called fisheyes take in incredibly wide areas, while the longest tele-photos can take full-size pictures of subjects hundreds of yards away.

Nowhere have computers been more import-ant than in the development of zoom lenses. These are lenses of variable focal length. When the lens is zoomed, the elements inside the lens move in relation to each other, and alter the bending power of the lens. The movement of the elements has to be very precise for the lens to work properly. Thanks to modern computer-aided design techniques, zoom lenses today can produce images every bit as good as those produced by lenses of fixed focal length.

As we have already seen, exposure is controlled by the intensity of the light coming through the lens and the length of time that the film is exposed to the light. The intensity of the light is governed by a diaphragm, which is basically a hole of adjustable size inside the lens. The size to which the diaphragm is opened is called the aperture and is measured in f. numbers, or "f-stops." The sequence f/2.8, f/4, f/5.6, f/8, f/11, f/16 is usually marked on the lens barrel of single lens reflex cameras. The lower the f-stop number, the greater the amount of light that is allowed to pass. Each of the f. numbers represents the same amount of light transmission whatever the focal length of the lens being used.

In the early days of photography, the intensity of light entering the camera was altered by inserting thin pieces of metal, called stops, punched with holes of different sizes into a slot in the lens barrel. Today, the variable diaphragm is built into the middle of the lens. With early SLR cameras, this was a problem. Because the photographer looked through the lens itself, the viewfinder image was very dim if a small aperture – that is, a high f. number – was used.

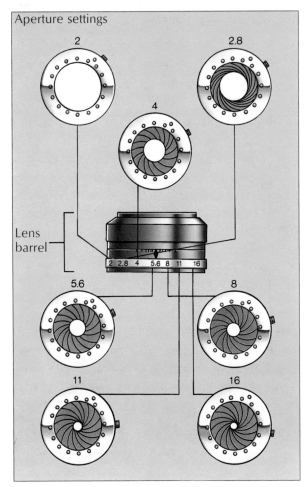

Aperture settings

Lens barrel

2 2.8 4 5.6 8 11 16

Below left F. numbers describe the size of an aperture. At f/2 the diaphragm is fully open.

Below A very shallow depth of field allows the subject of the photograph to stand out.

To achieve such great depth of field (everything from the foreground to the horizon is in focus) a small aperture was set.

This meant that the photographer had to compose the picture at the largest aperture available and then set a smaller aperture just before taking the picture. Today, this is all done automatically. The viewfinder shows the scene at maximum aperture, no matter what aperture has actually been set. The instant the shutter release is pressed, an electronic signal is sent to the diaphragm to set it to the aperture required.

Aperture settings have one very important consequence for photography: they change a picture's depth of field. Depth of field is the distance between the nearest and farthest points of a subject that appear to be in focus. With large apertures, depth of field is much shallower than with small apertures. Consequently, the diaphragm is very important in the creative process of taking the picture: by changing the aperture, the photographer can totally change the appearance of the photograph. For example, if you were photographing a crowd of people using deep depth of field, everyone in the crowd would be in sharp focus; using shallow depth of field, you could isolate a group of faces within the crowd by bringing them into focus.

Just as the diaphragm changes the intensity of light, the shutter alters the duration of the exposure. In early photography, when exposures often lasted several minutes, shutters were simple affairs. A popular design featured a moving blade with a hole cut in it; when the shutter release was pressed, the blade moved across behind the lens, allowing light to reach the film while the hole was in the light path.

Improvement in the light sensitivity of film, however, meant that shorter and shorter exposures could be made. In the early part of this century the lens, or leaf, shutter became the most common type of shutter. Lens shutters are circular in shape, with interleaving metal blades that open outward before closing again.

The very fast shutter speed used here has even frozen the water droplets in mid-air.

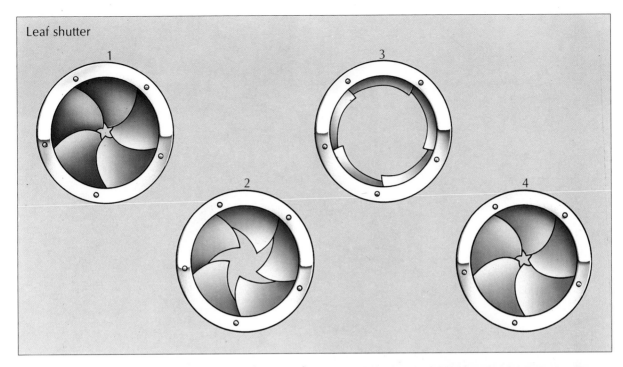

Leaf shutter

Above Lens, or leaf, shutters are made up of overlapping metal blades that open and then close again to make the exposure. Modern lens shutters are found in compact cameras, but are not used in SLRs.

Right Slow shutter speeds are often used to produce trick effects like this. Because the soldier has moved during the exposure, his outline has been blurred.

They are usually placed between the lens elements, and so they have the advantage of being quite small.

Although they are common in modern compact cameras, lens shutters are not really suited to reflex viewing systems. First, with a basic lens shutter, the photographer would not be able to see anything through the viewfinder until the exposure was actually made, because the shutter would be closed. Equally important, every lens for use with an SLR would have to incorporate its own shutter, which would make it more expensive to produce. The problem was finally solved by placing the shutter in the camera body.

The focal plane shutter of the Minolta Dynax 8000i is capable of an exposure lasting just 1/8000 second.

These shutters are known as focal plane shutters and are used in 35mm SLRs today. Focal plane shutters consist of a pair of metal blinds positioned behind the reflex viewing mirror and in front of the film. When the shutter release is pressed, the mirror is flipped up out of the light path and the two blinds move across the film. The film is exposed in the short space of time between the first blind's moving out of the light path and the second blind's blocking off the light again. The diagram on page 27 will make this clear.

Focal plane shutters are capable of extremely fast exposures (cameras such as the Nikon F-801 and the Minolta 8000i have maximum shutter speeds of 1/8000 second), which makes them ideal for "freezing" moving subjects. To achieve these fast speeds, the second shutter blind actually starts moving across the film plane before the first one has finished moving. This means that at fast shutter speeds the shutter is never fully open. The frame of film is exposed as the thin slit between the blinds moves across it. Although this makes very fast shutter speeds possible, it does present problems when flashes are used, as we will see in Chapter 15.

Focal plane shutter

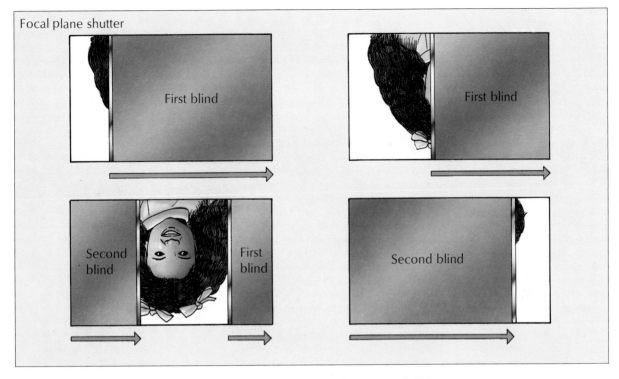

Above Focal plane shutters operate at extremely high speeds – up to 1/8000 second. The first blind starts to move across the film plane (top left and right); the second blind starts to move before the first one has finished moving (bottom left); the second blind blocks out the light again (bottom right).

Left Night photographs often require exposures lasting several seconds or even minutes. Many modern cameras allow the photographer to program the length of the exposure before the picture is taken and automatically hold the shutter open for that time.

27

10 Focusing systems

Focusing is the means by which a sharp, recognizable image is formed on the film. Manually focused lenses require the photographer to turn a focusing ring on the lens barrel which moves the lens closer to or farther away from the film, until the most important part of the scene is in sharp focus. Subjects very close to the camera require a longer lens-film distance than far-off ones.

Focusing is one of the more difficult aspects of photography, so camera manufacturers have made great efforts to develop automatic focusing systems. These range from the very simple, to systems that use the most advanced technology in modern photography.

The first autofocus camera was the compact Konica C35, which was launched in 1977. Since then many different autofocus compacts have

"Soft-focus" is produced by fitting a special glass filter over the lens.

been produced. Nearly all of them use an active autofocus system. An infrared beam is sent out by the camera as the lens begins to move from close focus to infinity. When a sensor on the camera receives a strong infrared reflection, the lens stops moving and the shutter is released. These active autofocus systems can be very efficient, but are limiting in certain ways. For example, it is not possible to take pictures through closed windows because the infrared beam is reflected by the glass. Consequently, many autofocus compacts now have a "land-scape" button to overcome this problem. This automatically sets the focus to infinity.

With SLRs, a passive type of autofocus system is used. Light coming through the lens is reflected by a mirror below the main viewing mirror, and is then split into two image-forming beams. These are directed at a "charged coupled device" (CCD), which is made up of hundreds of sensors called "arrays." The camera's electronic circuitry can analyze where the two beams are falling on the CCD and, therefore, whether the picture is in focus or not. If it is not in focus, signals are sent to the focusing motor, which moves the lens backward or forward until the beams are falling in the correct position on the CCD. This means of setting focus is sometimes called a phase detection autofocus system.

Early autofocus systems had difficulty with moving subjects, but the latest generation of autofocus SLRs, such as the Minolta Dynax 7000i, have "predictive" autofocus systems. As the subject moves, the lens is continually adjusted; when the shutter release is pressed, the camera is able to predict where the subject will have moved to in the time it takes for the viewing mirror to move out of the way and the shutter to open.

Above Infrared autofocus systems will focus on a pane of glass rather than on the scene beyond it unless the photographer pushes an override button.

Left The earliest passive autofocus systems could not always focus in low light, since there was not enough contrast in the scene for them to work. Consequently, the latest autofocus SLRs incorporate an infrared device that projects a pattern of infrared radiation onto the subject, allowing the autofocus system to function correctly.

We have seen how regulating shutter speed and aperture can give exactly the right exposure to the film. But there also has to be some means of knowing how much exposure is required. The camera's light metering system supplies this information.

In nineteenth-century photography, knowing how much exposure was needed was often a matter of experience. Gradually, mechanical exposure aids began to appear. One of these was the actinometer, a device that contained a reel of light-sensitive paper. The actinometer would be exposed to the light striking the subject, and the paper would begin to darken. The time that it took the paper to become a standard gray color was measured, and this was converted into apertures and shutter speeds.

Devices such as the actinometer were phased out with the development of the photoelectric cell in the 1930s. Photoelectric cells convert light intensity into an electric current; by measuring the current produced, it is possible to work out the exposure. Photoelectric cells were often bulky, and it was not until the 1960s that cadmium sulfide cells began to be produced. Because they are much more sensitive to light, they could be made much smaller.

Nearly every modern 35mm camera has a miniature metering cell built into it to measure the strength of light. The information gathered by the cell is used by the camera's computer to work out recommended shutter speeds and apertures. These are either shown in the viewfinder by light-emitting diodes (LEDs) or used to set the exposure automatically.

There are many different metering systems. One of the most common is center-weighted average metering, which takes a reading from the whole frame but puts extra emphasis on the center. This is because the main subject is likely

Actinometers contained paper that became darker with exposure to light. The speed with which the paper darkened was used to calculate shutter speeds and apertures, represented by the figures around the side of the dial. Nowadays, photographers use light meters that have photoelectric cells that gauge the amount of available light.

to be located in the middle of the photograph. Some of these systems take a reading that is biased toward the bottom half of the frame, because the sky is usually brighter than the ground. If the sky formed a large part of the picture, a reading taken at the center of the frame would result in an exposure too short for the ground to be recorded accurately.

A bright background can cause the main subject to be underexposed.

Other metering systems include spot metering, by which a light measurement is taken from a very small section at the center of the frame. Evaluative metering, which is found on the most modern 35mm SLRs, involves taking readings from something like six separate areas of the frame, which are analyzed by the camera's computer. Thousands of typical lighting conditions that occur in different picture-taking situations are stored in the computer's memory. When the computer finds a situation in its memory that resembles the readings it has just received, it is programmed to set specific exposure values automatically.

Spot metering is most useful when accurate exposure is needed for just a small part of a scene.

As we have already seen, exposure is determined by the size of the aperture and the shutter speed. The way in which apertures and shutter speeds are measured may seem a little strange at first. Apertures, for instance, progress in the sequence f/2.8, f/4, f/5.6, f/8, f/11, f/16, f/22, f/32. The aperture set at each f. number admits half the amount of light admitted by the f. number that comes before it. In the same way, a shutter speed of 1/30 second admits twice as much light as a shutter speed of 1/60 second, which in turn gives twice the exposure of 1/120 second. These numbers that denote shutter speed and aperture are used by all camera manufacturers, and are sometimes referred to as "stops." Reducing the aperture by one stop (from f/11 to f/16, say) has exactly the same effect as increasing the shutter speed by one stop (from 1/125 second to 1/250 second). This constant relationship between aperture and shutter speed is known as reciprocity.

The principle of reciprocity, together with camera manufacturers' ability to make metering cells small enough to be built into cameras, have made automatic and semi-automatic setting of exposure possible. With semi-automatic exposure, the photographer sets both aperture and shutter speed, but is able to see in the

Automatic exposure calculates the correct shutter speed and aperture — making it easier to photograph a scene with both bright and dark areas.

Above With automatic exposure, the photographer can set a fast shutter speed for exciting sports shots like this and rely on the camera to select the correct aperture.

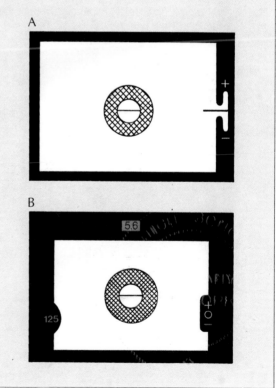

Aperture and shutter speed are shown in different ways in viewfinders: a needle moving on a scale (A); or a LED display (B).

viewfinder if the chosen settings give an exposure that matches the one recommended by the camera's metering cell. If they do not, the photographer adjusts either the aperture or shutter speed. These viewfinder exposure aids can be either mechanical – a bar that moves until it is lined up with a circle – or electronic – LED displays, lighting up in the viewfinder.

This system is still not very quick and has been largely replaced by automatic exposure setting. Here, the photographer sets either the aperture (aperture priority exposure) or the shutter speed (shutter priority exposure), and then the camera automatically selects the correct shutter speed or aperture, respectively. In other words, the photographer sets one, and the camera sets the other. The great advantage of automatic exposure is that it is easy to use while still allowing the photographer total control over such things as depth of field.

13 ◇ Programmed exposure

The logical development of automatic exposure is a system in which the camera sets both the aperture and the shutter speed automatically. This is called programmed exposure. Using information from the metering cell, the camera decides on a suitable combination of the two values. Thanks to the great advances in electronics over the last ten years, programmed exposure is now a feature of virtually every 35mm compact camera. On inexpensive compacts, the systems are often very simple. For instance, there may be only two apertures and two shutter speeds available for the camera to choose. More advanced compacts, however, have a wide range of shutter speeds and apertures.

Programmed exposure has also become increasingly common on the SLR in the last few years. On top models, it is usually provided along with automatic and semi-automatic exposure modes, and there is sometimes even more than one program. The reason for this is that normal programs are designed to choose medium apertures and shutter speeds. There are times, however, when the maximum depth of field is needed in the picture, so a small

The best autofocus SLRs will automatically bias exposure toward the area of the frame containing the subject.

Portrait exposure mode automatically selects a large aperture to isolate the subject.

aperture would be required. Similarly, a sports photographer needs to use the fastest shutter speed possible in order to "freeze" a moving subject and prevent the motion from blurring the picture. For these reasons, special depth and action programs are to be found on a number of SLRs.

The rapid advances in electronics have meant that camera programmed exposure systems are constantly being improved. The latest SLRs, such as the Minolta Dynax 8000i and the Canon EOS 10, use electronics to link up the autofocus and exposure controls. Information from the autofocus sensor about the position of the subject in the frame is fed to the exposure system. The exposure is then biased toward this area of the picture.

Both of these cameras also have special systems for controlling every aspect of the picture. Computer chips on cards are slotted into the Minolta Dynax 8000i. These direct the autofocus and exposure systems and even the motorwind, setting up the camera for specific picture-taking situations, such as portraits, landscapes and sports photography. The Canon EOS 10 comes with a booklet filled with photographs, with bar codes underneath each one. A bar code reader is run across the code, and the information in it programs the camera to reproduce the effect of the photograph in the booklet, such as "slow sync flash." The shutter speed is slow enough to record the background of the picture, which is unlit because it is too far away, as well as the flashlit foreground.

We have seen how electronics have revolutionized the camera. Many of the decisions that have to be made when taking a photograph are now taken care of automatically by the camera's computer. Cameras have also become a lot smaller and easier to handle. None of these things would have been possible without the great advances that have taken place in film technology. Today's films are often able to produce good results even when the picture's exposure is inaccurate.

On page 10, it was explained how Fox Talbot and Daguerre invented different methods of fixing images produced by their cameras. Pictures produced by Daguerre's process, called daguerreotypes, were positive images formed on copper plates that had been treated with a light-sensitive emulsion. The quality of daguerreotypes was very good for the time, but copies could not be made from them. Fox Talbot's calotypes, on the other hand, were negatives. Any number of positive prints could be made from each negative. The negative was held against a sheet of light-sensitive paper and exposed to light to produce the positive image.

This division between negative and positive images still exists today; films that are designed to produce prints on paper are negative films, while positive films give transparencies (slides). The way in which the image is recorded is, however, far more advanced than it used to be.

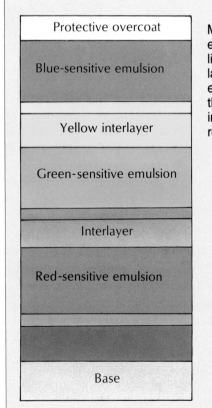

| Protective overcoat |
| Blue-sensitive emulsion |
| Yellow interlayer |
| Green-sensitive emulsion |
| Interlayer |
| Red-sensitive emulsion |
| Base |

Modern color films contain three separate layers of emulsion, with each one sensitive to red, green or blue light. When the film is developed, dyes in each of the layers appear in those parts of the film that have been exposed to the light. These three layers of dye make up the finished color negative image, which is then reversed in the printing process. The final color print is an accurate record of the subject.

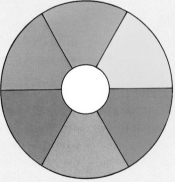

This color wheel shows the three primary colors in light – blue, green and red – to which the layers in color film are sensitive; opposite each of them is their complementary color – yellow, magenta and cyan – the colors of the dyes that appear during the course of developing the film.

The coarse grain in this photograph is caused by the film containing large silver halide crystals. Films of this type are sometimes used to give an artistic effect.

Early black-and-white photographs were usually produced on metal or glass plates; nowadays, clear celluloid is used. The celluloid usually comes in rolls and is coated with a layer of emulsion containing silver halide crystals, which are sensitive to light. Although this method of producing photographs has been known for decades, the technology involved has improved dramatically. In the past, large crystals of silver halide were required when photographing in poor lighting conditions because they are more highly sensitive to light. It is now possible to produce very small silver halide crystals that are still sensitive to light. This means that the films allow short exposure times without becoming "grainy." The "grainy" effect is caused by the coarse crystals or by crystals that clump together.

To produce color pictures, the early photographers simply tinted black-and-white photographs with oils and water-colors. Many different ways of producing real color photographs were explored, but it was not until the 1930s that a really practical system was devised. It is the one that is still used today, although in a greatly improved form. Color films are coated with three very thin layers of emulsion, which are sensitive to blue, green and red light. When the film is developed, chemicals called dye couplers in each layer produce dyes in the areas where the silver halide crystals have been exposed to light. The different colors in the three layers combine to form a full color picture.

One of the most important features of any film is its sensitivity to light. The more sensitive it is, the shorter the exposure needs to be. A film's sensitivity, or film speed, is nowadays described by an ISO number. The most commonly used films have ISO numbers of 100 or 200; fast films, which are more sensitive, have higher ISO numbers, such as ISO 400 or even ISO 3200. Slow films go right down to such film speeds as ISO 25.

Above Fast films enable photographers to take pictures in low light without the need for long exposures or flash light.

Below Polaroid cameras develop pictures instantly.

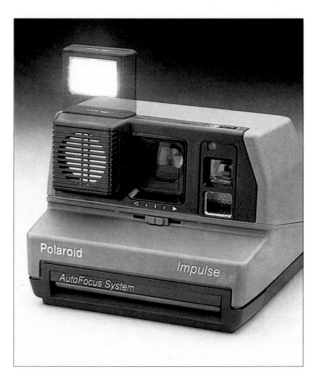

Infrared films are sensitive to invisible infrared radiation. They reproduce scenes in unusual colors.

The photographer must decide which film speed is best for a given situation. In low light or when moving subjects are being photographed, a fast film is usually chosen because it allows short exposures with shutter speeds fast enough to freeze movement. When the light is bright or when the length of the exposure is not important a slower film is preferable, because its grain is less noticeable and it provides sharper detail.

Until a few years ago, the photographer had to set the film speed using a dial on top of the camera. This allowed the metering system to show the correct exposure for the particular film being used. Nowadays, however, film speed is usually set automatically, by a system called DX coding. A pattern of black and silver squares on the film canister is "read" by contacts in the camera, and the computer converts the information into a film speed. The DX pattern provides other information, such as the number of pictures that can be taken on the roll of film and the film's tolerance – that is, how much it can be over- or under-exposed and still produce an acceptable picture.

The Polaroid system of instant film developing was invented in 1948. When the American Edwin Land's daughter complained to him that she could not see the pictures he had taken right away, he set about inventing an instant picture camera. In 1948, his Polaroid Corporation produced the first camera of this type, the Model 95. The exposed film was "sandwiched" with a developer inside the camera to produce a picture within one minute. Fifteen years later, in 1963, the first Polaroid camera to take instant colour pictures appeared. The film process remains the same today, but, of course, the cameras themselves have become more and more sophisticated.

Working with flash

Early photographic materials had very poor sensitivity, so it quickly became apparent that artificial lighting would be a great help to photographers. The problem with using electrically supplied light was that it produced a great amount of heat. People having their portraits taken would soon become very hot under the glare of the lights. Flash powder could be used instead. This consisted of magnesium and other chemicals, which were ignited by a spark to produce a burst of light. The camera's shutter had to be opened before the powder was ignited and closed again immediately afterward. A good deal of smoke and ash was produced in the process.

Flash lighting is now produced in a much more efficient and cleaner way. Batteries inside the flashgun, or the camera's own batteries, charge capacitors, which store electric current.

When the flash is fired, these capacitors discharge through a flash tube filled with special gas, producing a burst of brilliant white light. Modern electronic flash units are small, reliable and can be used over and over again.

As the light from the flash lasts only a fraction of a second – as little as 1/30,000 second with some flashguns – it is very important that the flash be synchronized to fire while the camera's shutter is fully open. Most compact cameras have flash units built into them, so the camera's electronic circuitry can fire the flash to coincide with the shutter opening. In many modern compact cameras, the flash will fire automatically if the metering system indicates that the light is too dim for a picture without a flash. Although some SLRs now have built-in flash units, most of them require separate flashguns. These are usually mounted on a "hot shoe" on

Early flash outfits were very bulky. The bulbs could not be used more than once.

Right One of the greatest problems when using flash is that people's eyes can appear red. This is because flash light passes through the subject's pupil and is reflected back to the camera by blood vessels at the back of the eye. To avoid "red-eye," some camera manufacturers have developed flash systems that flash several times before the picture is taken. The flash bursts cause the pupils to contract, reducing the amount of light that can be reflected.

Below With most SLRs, flash is provided by detachable units that are mounted on the camera's "hot shoe."

top of the camera. Electrical contacts in the hot shoe discharge the flash light when they receive a signal that the shutter is fully open.

However, SLRs cannot synchronize flash throughout their shutter speed range because of their focal plane shutters. At the faster shutter speeds – usually 1/125 second or faster – the shutter blinds are never completely open. Instead, an open slit between the two blinds is traveling across the frame of the film. This means that when the short burst of flash is produced, part of the frame will be obscured by the blinds and will not receive any light.

The Japanese company Olympus recently devised a means of overcoming this difficulty. They developed a special stroboscopic flash-gun, which gives a very rapid sequence of separate flash bursts. This means that every part of the film frame receives light from at least one of the bursts. Shutter speeds of up to 1/2000 second can be used with this flashgun.

Until recently, exposures with flash were controlled simply by altering the camera's aperture. The closer the main subject was to the camera, the smaller the aperture that was set. With non-automatic cameras, this could involve some quite complicated calculations. But the precision of the modern camera's electronic circuitry has made it possible to produce more accurately exposed flash photographs. When the flash is fired, a sensor on the front of the camera or the flashgun (or, with some SLRs, inside the camera body behind the lens) measures the flash light being reflected back to the camera. When the correct amount of light to produce an accurate exposure has been received, the flash is stopped. Since flash bursts usually last between 1/1000 second and 1/30,000 second, systems of this kind have to perform at lightning speeds.

Despite the arrival of still video cameras, the trends that have made photography what it is today seem set to continue. The camera's electronic systems seem likely to take more and more of the photographic decisions automatically, while allowing the photographer to override them when necessary. The pioneering technology of cameras such as the Minolta Dynax 7000i is almost certain to be incorporated into less expensive models, with autofocus, metering and programmed exposure all being linked to provide "intelligent" electronic control of all the camera's functions.

As far as lenses are concerned, zooms with ever-increasing focal length ranges are the way of the future. The SLR's interchangeable lenses will probably become less important as one zoom lens will offer virtually every focal length a photographer could need.

One of the major difficulties in photography at the moment is camera shake, to which heavy telephoto lenses are particularly vulnerable. With exposures longer than about 1/60 second, pictures can be blurred by the shaking of the camera in the photographer's hands during the exposure. This means the camera usually has to

Systems being developed could eliminate the problem of camera shake.

Above Modern communications systems allow pictures to be transmitted electronically worldwide.

be supported on a tripod for long exposures. However, prototype lenses that avoid this problem have already been designed. Canon's Image Stabilization Lens prototype features a pair of accelerometers that can detect movement or vibration. These pass information to an actuator that moves the position of elements inside the lens to keep the image steady.

Another way in which camera shake can be combatted is by doing away with the need for slow shutter speeds altogether. As film technology develops, faster and faster films with reduced grain will appear. Moreover, as film quality improves, films may get smaller in size. Negatives will not need to be so large if they can be enlarged without serious deterioration of the quality of the picture. Smaller film sizes in turn mean smaller cameras. In years to come, the 35mm SLRs may be thought of as the heavy, bulky relics of a bygone age, in much the same way that view cameras are today.

Above The cameras of the future perhaps. A still video camera system like this one combines a video camera, lens and transmitter.

Glossary

Accelerometer. A device that detects movement or vibration.

Actuator. A component that causes elements in the lens to change position.

Aperture. The size to which a camera's diaphragm is opened; measured in f. stops. This figure is arrived at by dividing the focal length in millimeters by the aperture in millimeters.

Bar code. A series of black and white lines that can be "read" by a scanner. A computer translates the lines into specific information.

Bellows. A lightproof sleeve of folded leather that links the lens, shutter and diaphragm with the back of a view camera. The bellows are flexible so that the lens can be moved backward and forward to focus the image.

Camera obscura. A darkened box with a small hole or a lens on one side. An upside-down image of the scene outside the box is formed on the inside opposite the hole or lens.

Camera shake. A problem that arises with long exposures. The camera moving in the photographer's hands while the shutter is open blurs the picture.

Capacitor. An electrical device that can store an electric charge.

CCD. A charged coupled device. The surface of this electronic component is sensitive to light.

Compact camera. Small and usually highly auto-mated camera with a non-reflex viewing system.

Depth of field. The distance between the nearest and farthest points of a subject that appear to be in focus. Depth of field is greatest at small apertures and with short focal lengths.

Developing. Treatment of exposed film with chemicals to produce either a negative or a positive transparency.

Diaphragm. The part of the camera that controls how much light passes through the lens. Most diaphragms are made up of overlapping blades that are adjusted to let in more or less light.

DX coding. A system for setting film speed automatically. A pattern of black and silver squares on the film canister is read by contacts in the camera's film loading compartment.

Elements. The individual pieces of glass in the camera lens.

Exposure. The combination of the intensity of light reaching the film and the length of time the film is exposed to the light.

Film. A roll or sheet of celluloid that has been treated with a light-sensitive material.

Flashgun. A unit that produces a burst of light to illuminate the subject of a picture.

Focal length. The distance between the lens and the point at which it focuses a distant image. Lenses of short focal length (wide-angle) cover a wider area than those of long focal length (telephotos).

Focusing. Moving the lens backward or forward until it produces a sharp and well-defined image on the film.

Frame. The area of a roll of film on which one exposure is made. It also refers to the area that can be seen through the camera's viewfinder.

Grain. The clumps of developed silver halide crystals that make up a photograph. Grain becomes more noticeable with higher film speeds and when big enlargements are made from a negative.

Hot shoe. The mounting on top of a camera where a flashgun is attached. Electrical contacts in the hot shoe link camera and flashgun.

Image. The picture focused by the lens on the film. It is also what is seen by the photographer in the viewfinder.

Infrared. Light is just one form of radiation. Infrared radiation is invisible but can easily be detected by sensors.

LED display. (Light Emitting Diode) An array of small flashing lights that are used to communicate information in the viewfinder.

Lens. The set of glass elements at the front of the camera that focuses light waves onto the film.

Light path. The route light takes through the lens and the camera body to reach the film.

Lightproof. Sealed to prevent the entry of light.

Light-sensitive. Light-sensitive materials are those whose chemical structure is altered by exposure to light.

Metering. Measurement of light intensity. Metering is used when setting exposures.

Negative. An exposed piece of film that, when developed, shows light tones as dark ones and vice versa.

Pentaprism. The characteristic "hump" on top of an SLR. It reverses the image produced by the lens from left to right, so what is seen on the left-hand side of the subject is also seen on the left-hand side of the viewfinder.

Print. A positive picture produced by printing a negative onto photographic paper.

Reciprocity. The constant relationship between aperture and shutter speed in producing the exposure.

Reflex. Involving the use of mirrors.

Shutter release. The button that is pressed to take a picture; it causes the shutter to open.

Single lens reflex (SLR). A camera that uses a reflex viewing system. With nearly every SLR, it is possible to change the lens on the camera body.

Still video. An electronic camera, in which the image is recorded by a CCD rather than on film.

Stops. The universally used figures that denote specific apertures and shutter speeds.

Stroboscopic. Flashing repeatedly at very short intervals.

Subject. The scene or person that is being photographed.

Synchronized. Occurring at the same time. In photography, flashguns have to be synchronized to fire while the camera's shutter is open.

Top plate. The uppermost surface of the camera, on which the shutter release and other controls are usually found.

Transparencies. Frames of developed film that show a positive image and therefore do not need to be printed.

Tripod. A three-legged stand to support a camera.

Viewfinder. The small window on the camera body through which the photographer looks to compose the picture. Different types of cameras have different viewfinder systems.

Zoom. A lens that can have various focal lengths.

Further reading

Czaja, Paul, *Writing With Light* (Chatham Press, 1973)

Dunn, Andrew, *Alexander Graham Bell* (Bookwright, 1991)

Fischer, Robert, *Trick Photography* (M. Evans, 1988)

The Magic of Black & White (Time-Life) (Silver, 1985)

Moon, G. J. *Photographing Nature* (C. E. Tuttle, 1970)

Owens-Knudsen, Vic *Photography Basics* (P-H, 1983)

Peach, S. & Butterfield, M. *Photography from Beginner to Expert* (EDC, 1987)

Index

Picture Acknowledgments

The publishers would like to thank the following for allowing their photographs to be reproduced in this book:

Allsport 14, 20, 24; Associated Press/Topham 43 (top); Canon UK Ltd 13; Mary Evans Picture Library 17 (top); Eye Ubiquitous *cover*, 19, 21, 22, 23, 25, 28, 29, 31, 32, 34, 35, 37, 38, 39, 41 (right), 42; Hasselblad 15; Hulton Picture Library 8 (top), 9; The Kodak Museum at the National Museum of Photography, Film and Television 10, 11, 12, 17 (bottom), 30, 40; Minolta UK Ltd 26; Nikon UK Ltd 16, 41 (left), 43 (bottom); Pentax UK Ltd 18; Polaroid UK Ltd 4, 38 (bottom); Science Photo Library 5 (bottom); Topham Picture Library 5 (top); Wayland Picture Library 8 (bottom); ZEFA 33.

Artwork by the Hayward Art Group.